cooking the SPANISH way

Paella is a delicious and impressive dish to serve for any occasion. (Recipe on page 26.)

cooking the

SPANISH way

REBECCA CHRISTIAN

easy menu
ethnic
cookbooks

Lerner Publications Company ■ Minneapolis

Series Editor: Patricia A. Grotts
Series Consultant: Ann L. Burckhardt

Photographs by Robert L. and Diane Wolfe
Drawings and Map by Jeanette Swofford

The page border for this book is derived from a pattern found on 15th-century Spanish tile.

To my mother and father,
with gratitude for all our gustatory adventures

Library of Congress Cataloging in Publication Data

Christian, Rebecca.
    Cooking the Spanish way.

    (Easy menu ethnic cookbooks)
    Includes index.
    Summary: Introduces the history, land, and food
of Spain and includes recipes for such dishes as
paella, arroz con pollo, gazpacho, and flan.
    1. Cookery, Spanish—Juvenile literature.
2. Spain—Juvenile literature. [1. Cookery,
Spanish] I. Wolfe, Robert L., ill. II. Swofford,
Jeanette, ill. III. Title. IV. Series.
TX723.5.S7C5   1982   641.5946   82-4709
ISBN 0-8225-0908-3 (lib. bdg.)

Manufactured in the United States of America

5 6 7 8 9 10 11 12 13 14 99 98 97 96 95 94 93 92 91 90

**Serve Spanish meatballs for an appetizer or main
course. (Recipe on page 36.)**

CONTENTS

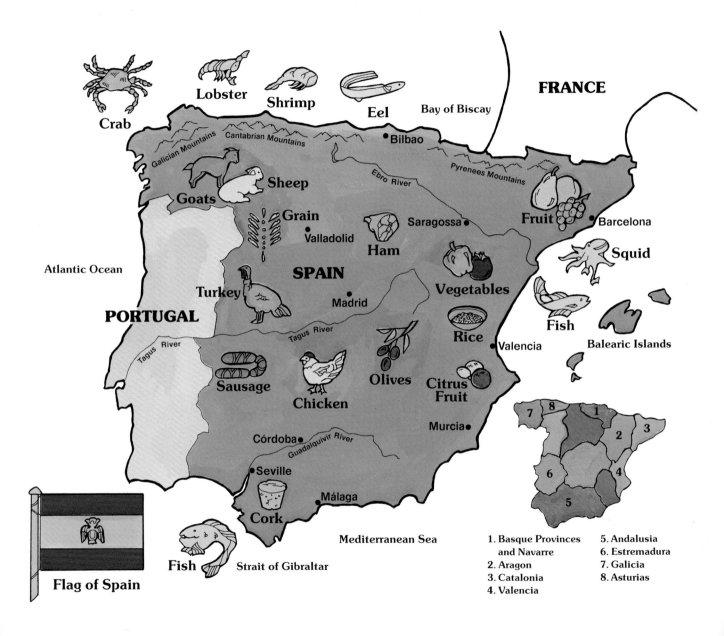

Crab

Lobster

Shrimp

Eel

Bay of Biscay

FRANCE

Galician Mountains

Cantabrian Mountains

Bilbao

Pyrenees Mountains

Ebro River

Saragossa

Fruit

Barcelona

Goats

Sheep

Grain

Valladolid

Ham

SPAIN

Vegetables

Squid

Atlantic Ocean

Turkey

Madrid

Fish

PORTUGAL

Tagus River

Tagus River

Rice

Valencia

Balearic Islands

Sausage

Chicken

Olives

Citrus
Fruit

Murcia

Córdoba

Guadalquivir River

Seville

Málaga

Mediterranean Sea

Cork

Fish

Strait of Gibraltar

Flag of Spain

1. Basque Provinces
   and Navarre
2. Aragon
3. Catalonia
4. Valencia

5. Andalusia
6. Estremadura
7. Galicia
8. Asturias

INTRODUCTION

Spain brings to mind the sound of castanets, the feel of the hot sun, the spectacle of the bullfight, and the taste of hot, spicy food.

You will find each of these things somewhere in Spain, but the large country is divided into many strongly contrasting areas. In some regions, it rains daily. In others, the climate is almost as dry as a desert. Styles of food from one region to another vary as dramatically as the climate. Whether it's succulent roast pork in Valencia, squid in the Basque country, or gazpacho soup in Andalusia, however, one characteristic is common to all good Spanish cooking. It uses the best, freshest ingredients. The country's history, land, and food have all contributed to the delicious varieties of cooking in Spain.

HISTORY

Known throughout its long history as "The Spains" because people of so many nationalities helped settle it, Spain is still regarded as enchantingly different than the rest of Europe.

Phoenicians, Celts, Greeks, Carthaginians, and Germans all left their mark on Spanish culture, but Romans and Moors were particularly important. They developed irrigation systems to fertilize the once arid lands where fruits and vegetables grow today.

The Moors conquered much of Spain in the eighth century, and it took the Spaniards 700 years to drive them completely out. In 1492, the same year that the Moors were finally defeated, Christopher Columbus sailed to North America. The curious Spaniards explored and eventually claimed Mexico, Central America, part of the southwestern United States, and much of both western South America and the West Indies. Explorers brought back tomatoes, potatoes, beans, corn, vanilla, chocolate, and eggplant, which provided new adventures in cooking at home.

By the late 1500s, however, distant foreign wars, bloody civil wars, and economic troubles lost Spain most of its empire. It remained a poor nation until only thirty years ago. Since then, investors drawn by business

opportunities and tourists lured by Spain's beauty have helped develop the country's economy. It has changed from an agricultural to an industrial nation.

THE LAND

Rising like a castle from the Atlantic Ocean and the Mediterranean Sea, square-shaped Spain dominates the Iberian Peninsula in southwestern Europe. After Russia and France, it is the third largest country in Europe.

Spain is barely linked to Europe through the lofty Pyrenees Mountains, which separate it from France. From the scorched hills of the south to the snowcapped mountains of the northeast, six regions compose Spain. The remote *Meseta,* an ancient, elevated table-land, covers half the country. It is bordered by Portugal on the west. Its poor soil is used for grazing and raising wheat. The *Northern Mountains* are also used for grazing. They stretch across the north, including the *Galician Mountains* to the west, the *Pyrenees Mountains* to the east, and the *Cantabrian*

Mountains in the central region. Irrigation has fertilized the windswept *Ebro Basin,* once a dry, desolate area. Stretching along the Ebro River in the northeast, it is bordered on the north by the Pyrenees Mountains, on the west and south by the *Meseta,* and on the east by low hills. Rivers irrigate the *Coastal Plains,* with rich, red soil extending along the Mediterranean Coast. The fertile *Guadalquivir Basin* follows the Guadalquivir River in southwestern Spain to the Atlantic. The sun-drenched *Balearic Islands* dot the Mediterranean Sea east of mainland Spain, making up the sixth land region.

THE FOOD

From tiny pink prawns to giant lobsters, seafood is the mainstay of Spanish cooking. The country is surrounded by water on three sides. Fishermen's catches are transported daily by truck, even to landlocked central areas. Beef is seldom served except in the northern pasturelands. Chicken, however, is important in the Spanish diet, as are fruits and vegetables. Olives, oranges, and grapes for wine are grown in large quantities.

Hills and streams separate Spain's 47 provinces, a fact which once forced Spaniards to stay close to home. Because of this isolation, the fiercely loyal people of each province developed their own cooking styles. Climate and available ingredients help characterize these styles.

In the restaurants of Madrid, Spain's centrally located capital, diners can sample foods from all regions. Variations of hearty stews made with pork, vegetables, and chick peas are cooked slowly in earthenware dishes over low heat. Stews originally became popular in Spain because they are easy to cook in one pot over primitive wood and charcoal stoves. The appeal of rich, strong stews lingers on even now that most people can afford modern stoves.

The rural areas outside Madrid parch in summer and freeze in winter. Few trees offer protection from the elements. Roasting of game is common here. Hunters prize wild boar, quail, turkey, pheasant, and deer. Suckling pig and baby lamb are also favorites.

Sparsely populated Estremadura, bordered by Portugal on the west, is famous for its spicy *chorizo.* This red sausage is used throughout Spain. Thin, wild asparagus cooked in butter is another Estremadura specialty.

In hot, dry Andalusia, a sparkling, fruity wine punch called *sangría* quenches thirst. Andalusian peasants were the first to create ice-cold *gazpacho* soup. This refreshing blend of tomatoes, garlic, cucumber, and green pepper is now a national favorite. Fish fried to a delicate crispness is another specialty.

The east coast of Spain is often called the Land of Rice. Rice is used in many dishes, particularly in *paella,* a savory rice stew of chicken, seafood, and vegetables. In addition to rice paddies, fragrant orange groves are found in eastern Spain.

Summer in Catalonia, a region in northeastern Spain, also brings fresh fruit to Spanish plates: juicy peaches, apricots, pears, cherries, and grapes all make excellent summer desserts, as do the many varieties of sweet melons found there.

Catalonian style food, which uses garlic liberally, is also popular in northeastern Spain and in France, across Catalonia's border. *Calamares,* which is squid, is a favorite from the Mediterranean Sea to Catalonia's east and south. It is served "in its own ink," a dark, pungent sauce. And seasonal foods enjoyed in Catalonia include the fall's wild wood mushrooms and the spring's fresh young vegetables.

In northeastern Spain, the ancient kingdoms of Aragon and Navarre are known for their sauces—ingredients such as tomato, onion, garlic, ham, and roasted fresh peppers are combined to make smooth and unforgettable accompaniments to many dishes.

In the Basque country to the west, the proud people have a deserved reputation for being passionate about food. Family ties are especially strong here, and gathering together in the dining room helps cement the bonds. Herbs are used skillfully and fish from the Bay of Biscay provide the inspiration for *sopa de pescado,* a savory fish soup. Tables groan under the weight of fowl, fish, meat, and vegetables—sometimes all served in different courses at the same meal.

Asturias and Galicia in northwestern Spain have cooking that resembles the cooking of Celtic Brittany and Normandy in France. To fend off the chill of the damp climate, rich and nourishing stews are eaten. A popular stew called *fabada* is made from a local white bean called *faba,* simmered with pork or ham. Because Galicia is Spain's most important fishing region, seafood stews are also eaten, often accompanied by spongy yellow cornbread. *Empanada* is another well-known dish of Galicia: a thick meat or seafood pie that is usually served cold.

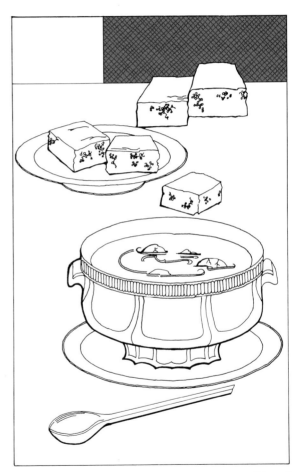

Seafood stew and cornbread make up a traditional Galician meal.

A shopper inspects the colorful fruits and vegetables at a typical Spanish open-air market.

A SPANISH MARKET

Most people in Spain shop every day. Although the modern cities in Spain have supermarkets, shopping almost always is done at specialty shops. Dairy products come from the milk bar, meat from the butcher, and vegetables from the produce stand. Most towns of any size have a large open-air market with a roof, but no walls, to protect it from the blazing sun. Amidst rows of purple eggplant, red tomatoes, and bright green lettuce, merchants compete for shoppers' attention. Chickens and many kinds of fish are sold *al fresco,* or natural, with their feathers, scales, eyes, and tails. Some chickens are so natural, in fact, that they are still alive—clucking and scolding about their unhappy fate. Merchants kill them right at the market to prove to customers that the poultry is very fresh.

Every market also has several rows of bright pink shrimp, mussels in striped shells, and tunas so big that they are cut into slices as thick as steaks. One fish, hake (hayk), is prepared by clamping its jaws onto its tail and frying it in a circle.

Olive oil is usually purchased daily at the market. This oil comes from the tasty green olives that are grown by the millions in southern Spain, and it is used throughout the country. Shoppers bring their own bottles to the market and fill them from an enormous container. There are almost as many kinds and qualities of olive oil as there are olives in Spain. Olive oil is used so often that many Spanish skillets never lose the smell of it, even when they are scrubbed clean.

THE SHEPHERD'S SUPPER

Today, more than half of Spain's people live in cities, and more Spaniards work in the manufacturing, construction, and mining industries than on farms. The standard of living in the cities has risen significantly since the 1950s, but rural life in Spain remains much the same as it did years ago. In the country, farmers live in small towns or villages and travel to the fields in donkey carts. Also, because most of Spain's land is used for pasture, shepherds are often seen tending flocks of goats or sheep.

When I was in Spain, I met a shepherd and shared a simple meal with him. I had been exploring a castle in eastern Spain and was walking down a narrow trail toward home when I met a herd of baaing sheep. Their shepherd was having his dinner on a big, flat white stone—a picnic table made for him by nature. *"¡Hola señorita!"* (OH-lah seen-yor-EE-tah), he called to me.

Because the shepherd rarely talked to anyone during the day, some of the sheep looked up in surprise at the sound of his voice. As I looked at the sheep, it was hard for me to imagine that the wooly lambs would one day be the delicious meat served in northern Spain.

The shepherd was wearing a black beret, a small hat that had not kept the sun and wind from his face. His friendly face was deeply tanned. He motioned me closer and offered to share his supper. In Spain, even strangers share food with each other.

The shepherd's supper was a small loaf of *pan* (pahn), or white bread, some chicken, a peach, an orange, cheese, and hearty red wine. It was not surprising that the shepherd was drinking wine with his meal. Although in North America we often think of wine as something to drink for a special occasion, in Spain it is served with every meal except breakfast. Spain does have expensive wines, but red table wine is very inexpensive. Young people in Spain may drink at a much earlier age than young people in North America, with their parents' full approval.

After finishing the chicken, which was

prepared very simply, the Spanish shepherd offered me a ripe, fragrant peach. I accepted it with thanks and looked in my backpack for my pocketknife. In Spain, it is considered bad manners to bite into a whole piece of fruit. Instead, Spaniards peel and chop the fruit into bite-sized pieces before they eat it. Some Spaniards are so used to preparing fruit in this way that they peel it very rapidly in one continuous motion. Before the shepherd and I started eating, however, we walked over and dipped our fruit in the nearby stream. Fruits are served unwashed in Spain, and at most dinner tables a bowl of cold water is passed to rinse them in. Spanish people believe this practice makes the fruit taste fresher.

The shepherd, like most Spaniards, ate his cheese for dessert. Cheese sometimes appears as an appetizer or in the Spanish version of the sandwich, but it is usually saved for the end of a meal. Most Spanish cheeses are white and smooth. One exception is *bolla* (BOY-yah), a robust orange cheese made from goat's milk.

After we finished eating, I thanked the shepherd and continued on my way. He raised his hand in farewell. Although his meal was a simple one, it was a delicious example of how good Spanish cooking can be. Many of the recipes in this book are simple, too, and only require certain special ingredients to give them the true flavor of Spain.

BEFORE YOU BEGIN

Cooking any dish, plain or fancy, is easier and more fun if you are familiar with the ingredients. Spanish cooking makes use of some ingredients that you may not know. Sometimes special cookware is used, too, although the recipes in this book can easily be prepared with ordinary utensils and pans.

Before you start cooking, carefully study the following "dictionary" of special ingredients and terms. Then read through the recipe you want to try from beginning to end. Now you are ready to shop for ingredients and to organize the cookware you will need. Once you have assembled everything, you can begin to cook. Before you start, it is also very important to read *The Careful Cook* on page 43. Following these rules will make your cooking experience safe, fun, and easy.

COOKING UTENSILS

double boiler—A utensil consisting of two saucepans fitting into each other so that any food placed in the upper pan can be cooked or heated by boiling water in the lower pan

food mill—A metal utensil with holes in it through which food is pressed

paella pan—A shallow, two-handled skillet used to make and serve *paella,* Spain's national dish. (Any large skillet can be used in place of this pan.)

spatula—A flat, thin utensil, usually metal, used to lift, toss, turn, or scoop up food

whisk—A small wire utensil used for beating food by hand

A *paella* pan

COOKING TERMS

boil—To heat a liquid over high heat until bubbles form and rise rapidly to the surface

brown—To cook food quickly in fat over high heat so that the surface turns an even brown

hard-cook—To cook an egg in its shell until both the yolk and white are firm

marinate—To soak food in a liquid in order to add flavor and to tenderize it

mince—To chop food into very small pieces

pinch—A very small amount, usually what you can pick up between your thumb and forefinger

Garlic and onions are often sautéed before they are added to other ingredients in a recipe. Here sautéed garlic and onions are lifted out of the pan with a spatula.

preheat—To allow an oven to warm up to a certain temperature before putting food in it

puree—To push food through a food mill or sieve or to whirl it in a blender to make a smooth, thick pulp called a *puree*

sauté—To fry quickly over high heat in oil or fat, stirring or turning the food to prevent burning

simmer—To cook over low heat in liquid kept just below its boiling point. Bubbles may occasionally rise to the surface.

A sharp knife is best for mincing food, but remember to be careful when using it.

SPECIAL INGREDIENTS

chorizo—A highly seasoned pork sausage

garlic—An herb whose distinctive flavor is used in many dishes. Fresh garlic can usually be found in the produce department of a supermarket. Each piece or bulb can be broken up into several small sections called cloves. Most recipes use only one or two finely chopped cloves of this very strong herb. Before you chop up a clove of garlic, you will have to remove the brittle, papery covering that surrounds it.

garlic salt—Dehydrated garlic combined with table salt

lentils—Brown, flat, dried beans

nutmeg—A fragrant spice, either whole or ground, that is often used in desserts

olive oil—An oil made from pressed olives that is used in cooking and for dressing salads

oregano—The dried leaves, whole or powdered, of a rich and fragrant herb that is used as a seasoning in cooking

Olive oil, garlic, garlic salt, peppers, and *chorizo* sausage are special ingredients used in Spanish cooking.

pimento—Small, sweet red chilies that come in cans or bottles and are often used to add color to food. The word is sometimes spelled in the Spanish way—*pimiento.*

red wine vinegar—A vinegar made with red wine that is often used with oil for dressing salads

saffron—A deep orange, aromatic spice made from the flower of the saffron plant

A SPANISH MENU

Below is a simplified menu plan for a typical day of Spanish cooking. The Spanish names of the dishes are given, along with a guide on how to pronounce them. Two alternate ideas for the main dish for dinner are included. Recipes for the starred items can be found in this book.

ENGLISH	ESPAÑOL	PRONUNCIATION GUIDE
Breakfast	**El Desayuno**	el deh-seye-YOO-noh
*Coffee with milk	Café con leche	kah-FAY kohn LEH-cheh
Rolls	Bollos	BOY-yohs
Dinner	**La Comida**	lah koh-MEE-duh
*Lentil soup Madrid style	Sopa de lentejas Madrileña	SOH-pah day len-TAY-hahs mah-dray-LAY-nyah
*Salad	Ensalada	ehn-sah-LAH-dah
*Paella or *Chicken with rice	Paella o Arroz con pollo	pah-EH-yuh oh ah-ROHTH kohn POY-yoh
*Stewed vegetables	Pisto manchego	PEE-stoh mahn-CHAY-goh
*Caramel custard	Flan	flahn
Appetizers/Snacks	**Tapas**	TAH-pahs
*Fruit punch	Sangría	sahn-GREE-yuh
*Spanish meatballs	Albóndigas	al-BON-dee-gahs
*Cucumber, tomato, and green pepper	Pepino, tomate, y pimiento	pay-PEEN-oh, toh-MAH-tay, ee pee-mee-EN-toh
Supper	**La Cena**	lah SEH-nuh
*Cold fresh vegetable soup	Gazpacho	gah-SPAH-choh
*Spanish omelette	Tortilla Española	tor-TEE-yah es-pahn-YOH-lah
Fruit	Frutas	FROO-tahs

BREAKFAST/
El Desayuno

Breakfast for most Spaniards is a very small meal. Some Spaniards don't have much more than a piece of bread or a roll and *café con leche* (coffee with milk) until the middle of the day.

Once I shopped for my morning pastry in a town so small that the bakery, which was in a row of houses, had no sign in front. The baker used the back part of her house for the bakery, or *panadería* (pah-neh-deh-REE-uh), and lived in the front. Since everyone in town knew her, there was no need for a sign. A villager pointed me in the right direction, and I found the bakery with my nose.

The bread is made fresh every day, brown and hard on the outside and soft and warm on the inside. A fresh roll hollowed out and filled with a few teaspoons of olive oil makes a between-meal treat for schoolchildren.

Because the bread is made without eggs and shortening, it becomes stale very quickly. But it tastes so good on the first day that it's made, it never lasts very long anyway. In fact, the butter and marmalade often served in restaurants and well-to-do homes are usually not even needed.

A typical Spanish breakfast consists of coffee and fresh-baked bread.

Coffee with Milk/
Café con Leche

Café con leche *is more milk than coffee and very heavily sugared. Most adults drink it, as well as some children.*

4 cups milk
4 teaspoons instant coffee
8 teaspoons sugar

1. In a saucepan, bring milk to a boil over medium heat, stirring constantly.
2. When milk begins to boil, turn off heat. Add coffee and sugar and stir until dissolved.
3. Serve Spanish style in 4 clear, heat-proof glasses.

Serves 4

DINNER/
La Comida

Between the hours of 2:00 and 4:00 P.M. in Spain falls the *siesta* (see-EHS-tah). Businesses close, schoolchildren are sent home, and working mothers and fathers rush back from offices and factories. At this time, the whole family eats a large meal of four to six courses.

The Spanish eat one course at a time. First comes the soup, then the salad, then the main course with potatoes, rice, or vegetables, and then the dessert. Adults often finish their meal with a cup of coffee, a glass of liqueur, or both beverages in the same cup.

After eating, many people rest. Although some say that fighting city traffic leaves very little time for napping, the custom remains strong in Spain. During *siesta* time, the usually noisy streets are silent.

Lentil Soup
Madrid Style/
Sopa de Lentejas Madrileña

1 **large onion, chopped**
1 **canned whole pimento, drained and chopped**
1 **green pepper, cleaned out and chopped**
4 **tablespoons olive oil**
2 **tablespoons all-purpose flour**
1 **16-ounce can (2 cups) tomatoes, cup up with a spoon**
3 **carrots, peeled and chopped**
2 **cups lentils (do not presoak)**
1 **tablespoon salt**
8 **cups water**

1. In a large kettle, cook onion, pimento, and green pepper in olive oil until soft.
2. Stir in flour. Then add tomatoes, carrots, lentils, salt, and water. Cover and simmer over very low heat for about 2 hours.

Serves 12

Sopa de lentejas Madrileña is a popular Spanish soup that is especially appealing in cool weather.

This *ensalada* often varies with the chef. Feel free to add a few extra ingredients, as the Spaniards do.

Salad/
Ensalada

½ head lettuce
1 hard-cooked egg, sliced
2 carrots, peeled and chopped
1 slice bologna, cut into small pieces
1 slice cheese (any kind), cut into
    small pieces
12 green olives (optional)
2 tablespoons vinegar
2 tablespoons olive oil
    pinch of salt
    pinch of pepper

1. Wash lettuce and pat dry with paper towels. Tear lettuce into bite-sized pieces and divide it among 4 small plates. (The Spanish do not use salad bowls.)
2. Put egg, carrot, bologna, and cheese on top of lettuce. Top with olives.
3. Mix vinegar, oil, salt, and pepper in a bowl. Pour 1 tablespoon of mixture over each salad.

Serves 4

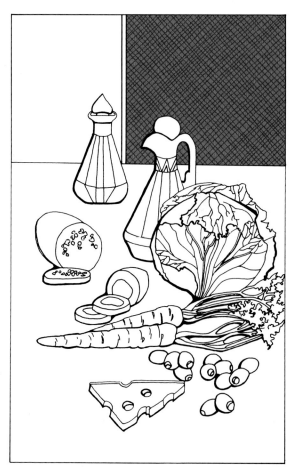

The above ingredients and salt and pepper are all that you need to make a delicious Spanish salad.

Paella

Paella *has no English translation. Served at nearly every home and restaurant, it is truly Spain's national dish. Spanish cooks make it in a shallow, two-handled black skillet called a* paella *pan. The pan is taken directly from stove top to table, where the dish is served by the person at the head of the table.*

12 small fresh clams in shells or ½ cup
    canned cooked clams
12 medium-sized fresh shrimp in
    shells or ½ cup canned cooked
    shrimp
8 ounces chorizo or other garlic-
    seasoned sausage
2 tablespoons olive or cooking oil
    a 2½-pound chicken, cut into 8
    serving pieces
2 15-ounce cans (about 4 cups)
    chicken broth
1 medium-sized onion, cut into
    wedges
1 sweet red or green pepper,
    cleaned out and cut into strips, or
1 canned whole pimento,
    drained and sliced
½ teaspoon minced garlic
2 cups white rice, uncooked
½ teaspoon oregano
¼ teaspoon saffron
½ cup fresh peas or ½ 10-ounce
    package frozen peas

1. *For fresh clams*—cover clams in shells with salted water using 3 tablespoons salt to 8 cups cold water. Let stand 15 minutes and rinse. Repeat soaking and rinsing twice. Set aside. *For fresh shrimp*—remove shells from shrimp. Split each shrimp down the back with a small knife and pull out the black or white vein. Rinse shrimp and dry on paper towels. Set aside.
2. In a *paella* pan or a very wide skillet, cook sausage 10 minutes or until done. Drain, let cool, and slice. Set aside.
3. Heat oil in the skillet and brown chicken 15 minutes, turning occasionally. Remove chicken and set aside.

4. In a saucepan, heat chicken broth to a boil. Meanwhile, brown onion, red pepper, and garlic in oil remaining in the skillet. Remove oven racks and preheat the oven to 400°.

5. Add rice, boiling broth, oregano, and saffron to the skillet. Bring to a boil over high heat and then remove.

6. Arrange chicken, sausage, shrimp, and clams on top of rice. Scatter peas over all. Set the pan on the oven floor and bake uncovered for 25 to 30 minutes or until liquid has been absorbed by rice. *Never* stir *paella* after it goes into the oven.

7. Remove *paella* from the oven and cover with a kitchen towel. Let rest 5 minutes. Serve at the table directly from the pan.

Serves 6

Arroz con pollo combines seasoned chicken with rice and juicy tomatoes.

Chicken with Rice/ Arroz con Pollo

1½ 15-ounce cans (about 3 cups)
　　chicken broth
¼ teaspoon saffron (optional)
　　a 2½-pound chicken, cut into 8
　　serving pieces
4 tablespoons olive or cooking oil
1 teaspoon paprika
½ teaspoon minced garlic
½ teaspoon oregano
1 large onion, chopped
½ cup sliced fresh mushrooms or 1
　　3-ounce can sliced mushrooms,
　　drained
1 cup finely chopped fresh
　　tomatoes or 1 8-ounce can (1
　　cup) tomatoes, cut up finely
　　with a spoon
1½ cups white rice, uncooked
½ teaspoon salt
　　freshly ground pepper to taste

1. Bring 1 cup chicken broth to a boil, sprinkle with saffron, and stir gently. Set aside.
2. Meanwhile, coat chicken pieces with mixture of 1 tablespoon oil, paprika, garlic, and oregano. Heat remaining 3 tablespoons oil in a large skillet with a lid. Sauté chicken pieces until golden. Set chicken aside on a platter.
3. Sauté onion and mushrooms in the skillet until onion is almost soft. Stir in tomato. Add rice and toss until coated.
4. Add chicken broth, chicken pieces, and salt and pepper. Bring to a boil, lower heat, cover, and simmer until chicken is tender and rice has absorbed liquid (20 to 30 minutes).

Serves 6

Pisto manchego makes a nutritious vegetarian main dish.

Stewed Vegetables/ Pisto Manchego

Vegetable dishes in Spain are often served as a separate course and sometimes as a main course. Pisto manchego *can be served in these ways and also as a side dish.*

To change this recipe, you can omit the potatoes and add 1 8-ounce package of frozen lima beans or 1 large chopped green pepper.

¼ **cup olive or cooking oil**
1 **medium-sized onion, sliced**
4 **small zucchini, sliced**
3 **medium-sized tomatoes, peeled
and chopped, or 1 16-ounce can
(2 cups) tomatoes, cup up with a
spoon**
2 **or 3 potatoes, peeled and quartered**
¼ **cup finely chopped fresh parsley**
1 **clove garlic, minced, or ½ teaspoon
garlic salt**

1. Heat oil in a large heavy skillet or deep pot. Add onion and cook until soft.
2. Add zucchini, tomatoes, potatoes, parsley, and garlic. Cover and simmer over low heat until vegetables are tender (about 30 minutes). *Pisto manchego* may be served hot or cold.

Serves 6

Caramel Custard/ Flan

You would have to look hard in Spain to find the cakes, cookies, and other sweet desserts that North Americans are used to. Although pastries are occasionally passed around at the end of a special meal, sweets are generally saved for an evening snack. Flan is a common dessert that is sweet but just light enough to handle after a large meal. It is usually baked with the sauce and inverted for serving. In this recipe, however, the sauce is prepared separately and poured over the top of the flan.

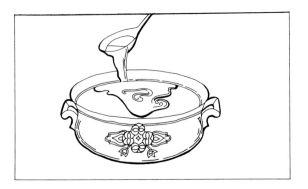

Custard ingredients:

2 cups milk
3 eggs, slightly beaten
¼ cup sugar
½ teaspoon vanilla extract

1. In a saucepan, warm 2 cups milk over low to medium heat for 10 minutes, stirring constantly. Set aside.
2. Preheat the oven to 325°.
3. In a large bowl, beat eggs, sugar, and vanilla with an eggbeater. Stir in warm milk.
4. Pour mixture into a 1-quart baking dish. Set the dish in a shallow pan of water and bake for 1 hour. (Custard is done when a knife inserted into it comes out clean.)
5. After custard has been baking for about 35 minutes, prepare sauce. (For a simpler version of sauce, melt 10 caramels in a saucepan over low heat. Add ¼ cup milk and stir constantly until completely blended (about 10 minutes). Pour sauce over flan and serve.)

Sauce ingredients:

3 egg yolks, beaten
¾ cup light cream
¾ teaspoon salt
½ cup brown sugar
3 tablespoons butter
1½ tablespoons lemon juice

1. Place first 4 ingredients in the top of a double boiler. Stir and cook *over,* not *in,* water boiling in the lower part of the boiler until mixture is thick and creamy.
2. Add butter and lemon juice a little at a time, stirring constantly.
3. Remove custard from the oven and pour sauce over the top. *Flan* may be served hot or cold.

Serves 4

Flan **can be prepared in a rectangular baking dish or a one-quart ovenproof bowl.**

APPETIZERS/SNACKS
Tapas

Spanish cafés are wonderful places in which to sit and talk or just watch people go by. The purchase of a single glass of wine or *anisette,* a drink that tastes like licorice, is a night's rent for a table in one of Spain's thousands of cafés. Many people spend an evening going from café to café, stopping to sample the *tapas*—bits of shrimp, egg, potato, and sausage—sold for a few *pesetas* a taste.

Fruit Punch/
Sangría

A common sight in Andalusia is people sitting at outdoor cafés sipping sangría. *This refreshing punch is typically made from wine, brandy, and fruit juice, but the following recipe substitutes extra fruit juice for the wine and brandy.*

Sangría is most attractive when served in a clear pitcher so that the floating orange and lemon slices can be seen. First drink the punch. Then dip into the bottom of your glass with a spoon to get the punch-soaked bits of fruit.

¼ **cup sugar**
1 **cup orange juice**
4 **cups grape juice**
½ **lemon, sliced**
½ **orange, sliced**
1 **small apple or peach, cut into thin wedges**
4 **cups club soda**
 ice

1. In a large pitcher, combine sugar, orange juice, and grape juice.
2. Add lemon, orange, and apple. Stir until sugar is dissolved.
3. Just before serving, add club soda.
4. Put ice cubes into 8 glasses. Pour *sangría* over ice and spoon some fruit into each glass.

Serves 8

Ice-cold *sangría* is perfect to sip on a hot summer day.

Spanish Meatballs/ Albóndigas

Meatballs in Spain are usually served as tapas, *but they also make a delicious light meal, especially when served with a vegetable or a salad and bread. For a more substantial meal, soup may be added to the menu.*

1 pound ground beef
4 ounces ground chorizo or other
       spicy sausage
¾ teaspoon salt
       dash of nutmeg
1 tablespoon finely chopped fresh
       parsley
2 slices bread, soaked in water
1 egg
3 tablespoons olive oil
1 cube beef bouillon (optional)
1 cup water (optional)

1. Combine meat, salt, nutmeg, and parsley in a large bowl.
2. Squeeze water from bread and add bread and egg to meat mixture. Form into about 36 small balls. In a frying pan, heat olive oil and sauté meatballs until thoroughly cooked and brown (about 20 minutes). Serve immediately. (If served as appetizers, provide toothpicks or party skewers.)
3. To keep meatballs warm in a thin sauce, dissolve 1 cube beef bouillon in 1 cup boiling water and pour over meatballs. Keep warm over low heat.

Serves 12 (as appetizer) or
6 (as main course)

Cucumber, Tomato, and Green Pepper/
Pepino, Tomate, y Pimiento

2 or 3 thin slices onion, chopped
1 tablespoon finely chopped fresh parsley
½ teaspoon salt
1 cup olive oil
1 large cucumber
2 medium-sized tomatoes
1 large green pepper
⅓ cup vinegar

1. Combine onion, parsley, and salt in a jar with a lid. Add olive oil and let stand 30 minutes.
2. Peel and slice cucumber into at least 16 circles. Cut each tomato into 8 wedges. Cut green pepper in half and clean out. Slice each half from top to bottom, making 8 strips. Then cut each strip in half to make 16 pieces. Put vegetables in a bowl.
3. Add vinegar to olive oil mixture. Screw lid on jar tightly and shake. Then pour dressing over vegetables. Refrigerate vegetables for at least 30 minutes before serving.
4. Center pieces of cucumber, tomato, and green pepper on toothpicks and serve.

Serves 8

SUPPER/ La Cena

Spaniards usually eat supper very late in the evening. Around 10:30 or 11:00 P.M., a light supper, much like a North American lunch, is served. It is usually some combination of salad, fruit, cheese, sandwiches, and soup. This hour sounds late for supper, but remember that the Spanish rest in the afternoon.

Cold Fresh Vegetable Soup/ Gazpacho

2 medium-sized cucumbers, peeled and chopped
5 medium-sized tomatoes, peeled and chopped
1 large onion, chopped
1 medium-sized green pepper, cleaned out and chopped
2 teaspoons finely chopped garlic
4 cups French or Italian bread, trimmed of crusts and chopped
4 cups cold water
¼ cup red wine vinegar
4 teaspoons salt
4 tablespoons olive oil
1 tablespoon tomato paste

1. In a deep bowl, combine cucumber, tomato, onion, green pepper, garlic, and bread. Mix together thoroughly.
2. Stir in water, vinegar, and salt.
3. Puree mixture in a food mill, working with 2 cups at a time. (If you've never used a food mill before, have an experienced cook show you how. When entire mixture has been pureed, discard any pulp left in the mill.) Beat olive oil and tomato paste into puree with a whisk.
4. Cover the bowl tightly with foil or plastic wrap. Refrigerate for at least 2 hours. Stir soup lightly just before serving.

Serves 6 to 8

Gazpacho, a spicy cold soup, can be served either as a first or main course.

Onions and potatoes make this Spanish omelette especially tasty.

Spanish Omelette/
Tortilla Española

A tortilla, or omelette, appears almost daily in a Spanish home. Spaniards eat the tortilla as a main dish at a light supper or as a side dish at the big midday meal. Slices of it can also be served as tapas. The omelette is good either hot or cold. Usually it is served hot and the leftovers are refrigerated for a snack. The nutlike flavor of the Spanish omelette comes from slowly cooking the potato and onion in olive oil. This unique taste is lost if any other kind of oil is used.

¼ **cup olive oil**
1 **large onion, minced**
1 **large potato, minced**
¼ **teaspoon salt**
5 **large eggs, beaten**
1 **tablespoon olive oil**

1. Heat olive oil in a frying pan over moderate heat. Add onion and potato and sprinkle with salt. Cook until soft, but not brown, stirring occasionally.
2. Add about one-third of beaten egg. Using a spatula, lift up omelette at the edges and center to allow egg to run under potato and onion. Repeat this procedure until all egg has been added.
3. When egg is firm but still slightly moist (not runny) and golden on the bottom, run the spatula under omelette to loosen it from the pan. Then place a plate over the top and flip omelette onto the plate. (You may want to have someone help you with this.)
4. Add another tablespoon olive oil to the pan and slide omelette back in, brown side up. Continue cooking omelette over moderate heat until golden on the other side.

Serves 2 to 4

A SPANISH TABLE

A Spanish table is often covered with a white linen tablecloth, and a vase of fresh flowers is placed in the middle. A pretty bowl or basket of colorful fruit, which grows so plentifully in Spain, can also give your table a Mediterranean look. Oranges, plums, lemons, peaches, or other fruit make attractive arrangements.

In Spain, the table is set with silverware, but the plates aren't added until it is time to eat. The food is dished up at the stove, one course at a time, and the plates are brought to the table after everyone is seated. With the exception of a *paella* pan, diners never see a serving dish.

THE CAREFUL COOK

Whenever you cook, there are certain safety rules you must always keep in mind. Even experienced cooks follow these rules when they are in the kitchen.

1. Always wash your hands before handling food.
2. Thoroughly wash all raw vegetables and fruits to remove dirt, chemicals, and insecticides.
3. Use a cutting board when cutting up vegetables and fruits. Don't cut them up in your hand! And be sure to cut in a direction *away* from you and your fingers.
4. Long hair or loose clothing can easily catch fire if brought near the burners of a stove. If you have long hair, tie it back before you start cooking.
5. Turn all pot handles toward the back of the stove so that you will not catch your sleeve or jewelry on them. This is especially important when younger brothers and sisters are around. They could easily knock off a pot and get burned.

6. Always use a pot holder to steady hot pots or to take pans out of the oven. Don't use a wet cloth on a hot pan because the steam it produces could burn you.
7. Lift the lid of a steaming pot with the opening away from you so that you will not get burned.
8. If you get burned, hold the burn under cold running water. Do not put grease or butter on it. Cold water helps to take the heat out, but grease or butter will only keep it in.
9. If grease or cooking oil catches fire, throw baking soda or salt at the bottom of the flame to put it out. (Water will *not* put out a grease fire.) Call for help and try to turn all the stove burners to "off."

METRIC CONVERSION CHART

WHEN YOU KNOW		MULTIPLY BY	TO FIND	
MASS (weight)				
ounces	(oz)	28.0	grams	(g)
pounds	(lb)	0.45	kilograms	(kg)
VOLUME				
teaspoons	(tsp)	5.0	milliliters	(ml)
tablespoons	(Tbsp)	15.0	milliliters	
fluid ounces	(oz)	30.0	milliliters	
cup	(c)	0.24	liters	(l)
pint	(pt)	0.47	liters	
quart	(qt)	0.95	liters	
gallon	(gal)	3.8	liters	
TEMPERATURE				
Fahrenheit	(°F) temperature	5/9 (after subtracting 32)	Celsius temperature	(°C)

COMMON MEASURES AND THEIR EQUIVALENTS

3 teaspoons = 1 tablespoon

8 tablespoons = ½ cup

2 cups = 1 pint

2 pints = 1 quart

4 quarts = 1 gallon

16 ounces = 1 pound

INDEX

ABOUT THE AUTHOR

Author **Rebecca Christian** acquired her taste for *paella* and other Spanish specialties while teaching English in Barcelona, Spain. Christian, a graduate of Iowa State University in Ames, has been a reporter for the Mason City (Iowa) *Globe-Gazette,* the public relations director for the State Library of Iowa, and an editor/writer at Rodale Press in Emmaus, Pennsylvania.

Christian now lives in Decorah, Iowa, where she writes on a freelance basis and teaches college courses and seminars in creative writing. She has authored four books and has written many magazine and newspaper articles, for which she has won a number of journalistic awards. In her spare time, Christian enjoys reading, camping, gardening, and cooking, and she often prepares recipes from *Cooking the Spanish Way* for her husband and two young children.

easy menu
ethnic
cookbooks

Pepino, Tomate, y Pimiento is a colorful and refreshing appetizer. (Recipe on page 37.)

641.594
C
Christian, Rebecca.

Cooking the Spanish way.

PINE TREE SCHOOL